Principles for Cyber Security Operations

Principles for Cyber Security Operations

Hinne Hettema

@themyops

Copyright © 2020 by Hinne Hettema.

ISBN (print)   9781660739226

Keywords: 1. Technology-Management, 2. Cyber security-operations 3. Cyber security-Incident Response 4. Cyber security-Business risk

Cover image utilises a modified icon representing a butterfly from The Noun Project, (2013), licensed under a Creative Commons attribution 3.0 licence. Obtained from

https://en.wikipedia.org/wiki/File:Butterfly_icon_(Noun_Project).svg

Table of Contents

PART I

The role of Principles

Security teams play a key role in the resilience against cyber-attack of their host organisations.

In the context of cyber security, resilience is defined as the capability to operate continuously in the face of an active and present (or lurking) adversary. This is the case for cyber security teams as well as physical security teams.

This book is focused on cyber security teams and the principles that drive robust cyber security operations and active defence. Cyber security operations are the activities that we undertake, every day, to ensure that business operations continue in a manner that is reliable, trustworthy and resilient.

Some cyber security operations work better than others. By that, we mean that they work more effectively, or are more aligned with what matters to the business in terms of people, process, revenue and technology.

My claim is that better functioning operations function better because they adhere to a sound set of *principles* in their operation. Adherence to principles matters, both in business and in personal life, especially as a marker of mastery in a particular area.

The idea for this book came from Ray Dalio's book *'Principles'* (Simon & Schuster, 2017). Dalio outlines a lot of the reasoning why principles are important in general and why and how they matter. This book is not a rehash of all that work. This small book must be read as a variation on the theme of principles – strongly focused on the principles that matter in the practice of operational security and active defence. Their scope is limited to that field.

The main reason why principles are important in cyber security is that a lot of organisations do cyber security really poorly. Principles – meaning the operational principles that can be implemented and supported by day to day security operations, almost regardless of levels of technical maturity, are the main tools to implement the mission and purpose of the security team.

Research done by Mandiant, and published yearly as the M-Trends report, indicates that security breaches have a 'dwell time' (time the attacker spends in the network undetected) counted in months. That means that intruders have a 'free reign' of months before they are discovered and are active for a long time in the environment before being noticed and evicted. This happens despite advanced technical tooling being readily available, so it points to something else that must be wrong.

These long dwell times point primarily to operational deficiencies: it is likely that the technical tooling to pick the compromise up was either not in place or not being looked at, despite it being readily available. The underlying reason for this lapse is that the implicit security posture present in far too many organisations assumes that intruders can be 'kept out' of the network indefinitely.

This security posture is implicit and has unconsidered operational consequences. A more robust and reliable approach is based on 'assumed breach' with a sound set of principles for security operations.

Purpose, posture and mission

The purpose of security operations is to ensure the continuity, integrity and availability of business operations in the face of ongoing cyberattack. Putting more definition around that requires that we look at things from the viewpoint of *adversaries*, especially the *failure modes* of adversaries. A robust set of security practices, driven by robust security principles, will allow an organisation to drive an attacker to their failure mode before they achieve their objectives.

Specifically, the aim of an organisation's defensive activities is to prevent an attacker from achieving their objectives at all times (and hence drive them into a failure mode). It is my belief that this is a defensible security posture for almost all environments. Notice how different this posture is from 'no attacker must ever get in', which is where many organisations are at.

Security posture is, in my view, an approach to security that is based largely on a number of presuppositions that in most places go unstated.

Poor security posture is specifically attributable to a lack of understanding of key operational business principles and a lack of understanding of their security context.

Taking these two as a combination, I propose that we adopt the following definition of security posture:

Definition: Security posture is the adaptation of existing, adopted and explicated operational principles to a cyber-security context.

While this may not be the entire story, it points at least to why security posture as a term is often so vague: most organisations only have implicit business operational principles, do not understand their security context, and use a hit and miss translation.

The notable aspect of the definition is that the security posture is driven by principles – business operational principles represented in a cyber security context. The principles in this book, especially numbers 1 through 6, are instrumental in understanding that context. Principle 7 in this book outlines how a security posture based on a solid understanding of actual threats faced by an organisation may be translated into strategy.

Most organisations that are lacking a defined security posture instead gravitate to a *default* posture which is implicitly adopted instead. This posture is likely the 'no attacker must ever get in' posture. The consequences of this posture are in almost all cases a reduction, not an improvement in the security capability. The fear that results from this approach leads to fatal miscalculations in almost all dimensions of operational security that really matter: people, culture, visibility and defence focus.

Aspect	Fear-based	Assumed breach
Security posture	Reactive	Proactive
Incident approach	Panic [denial, anger, bargaining]	Controlled chaos
HR	"we need a fall guy"	"build the team"
Security monitoring	Haphazard or Vendor driven	Controls based on Attacker behaviour Exploit risks Vulnerability Exposure
Predictability	None / little	Anticipated events
People impact	Burn-out	Busy
Security perception	IT problem	Business problem
Perception of hackers	Hackers are nerds doing bad things	Hackers are people too
Defence focus	Border Fortress Defence in depth	"Assume breach" Immune system Resilience

Table 1: The cost of not having a defined security posture: fear, blame, high costs, vendor lock in and compromise.

What I am suggesting is that the lack of stated business principles together with a faulty understanding of the security context is likely to lead to a security posture based on fear: a hope and pray security approach coupled to a Hollywood version of a hacker. This is the security model that we already know doesn't work.

It is the purpose of operational principles to embed the modes of thinking that get us past the 'default' strategy and onto a winning strategy, where the organisation is resilient against attack.

Goals of security operations

A successful security operation will achieve organisational resilience through a smart combination of the following four specific goals:

1. Minimising dwell time to the point where attackers are incapable of achieving their objectives
2. Limiting lateral movement of attackers on the network
3. Preventing re-entry into the network after closure of an incident
4. Understanding attacker motivation and capability where possible. Do not get caught in the 'attribution game'.

The principles in this book are key tools to achieve these goals. They are the ones that I believe are widely shared in the community of security people with relevant experience, and they are certainly the ones that have worked for me.

What about maturity?

I contrast principles to maturity. Security people like to say security is a journey. If it is, we need principles to guide us along the path, rather than maturity, which induces stasis. Security practices cannot afford stasis.

There are a number of reasons why it's better to focus on the principles of security operations than on the maturity model for security operations. They are:

1. Maturity models are based on a fixed end-goal. This is generally a poor match for security, which is best based on an ongoing process of improvement of practices based on a robust understanding of current attacks and their motivations (see principle 7, Strategy is bottom up).

2. Hackers are smart, and move quickly. 'Maturity' is a poor match for the sort of adversarial landscape that cyber security operations face daily.
3. Maturity models propose a single road or roadmap to improve maturity. This does not match the variety of business needs and associated security postures that security needs to implement. Moreover, security teams need to be agile in order to quickly adapt to and engage with attackers.
4. A known security end-state is incapable of adapting to and incorporating relevant new technologies. A lot of the best security work is done first in open source projects, which deliver real benefits; yet it is hard to adopt such software when the focus is on static roadmaps.

The purpose of the principles

The principles that follow are not based on technology, but instead capture the unique culture of exploration, agility, feedback, excitement and innovation that characterise the best security teams.

The idea is that operational security done well strives for high visibility, has very strong boundaries around that visibility, closes the incident loop to the point where they understand attackers, and work actively to change their organisations for the better.

At times the book may seem preachy, and it is indeed somewhat of a sermon. That is not because I claim to know everything. It is because I believe that these principles will allow an organisation to understand what is true about their security risks. Facing up to reality is the first step of real improvement.

These principles are what I believe is true about security operations. I have seen them work in practice multiple times, and at the times I deviated from them, there has been a price to pay.

The principles here can avoid costly mistakes in setting up and running a security capability. The best security teams I know have made them their own. I may have missed some. Where I have, develop your own.

PART II: Principles for Security operations

1

Visibility: Go by what there is, not by what there should be

Intruders look at a situation as they find it. The tooling they use, network scanning, probing and lateral movement, is based on facts and realities on the ground. A system is vulnerable or it isn't. A port is open or it isn't. An administrator left their password in a file on the network or didn't. There is no try.

Therefore it is critical that security teams go by what they see. In this sense, security teams are like attackers and think like attackers. This does not always go down well with the rest of the organisation.

A corollary of this view is that reports should always be truthful and not 'managed' (by which I mean that the information they contain is massaged to fit perceived or politically desirable, rather than actual, reality). The drive to 'manage' a report is often masked by a desire to ensure that only 'relevant' data gets reported; where 'relevant' is of course defined by what matches desire and perception. Security teams should stand firm in the face of these pressures. Making these sort of concessions always leads to situations where the true picture is lost to a form of fantasy.

Everything is visible and measurable

One of the early benefits of having robust security operations is that it enhances visibility in the environment, exposes things that go wrong, and assists with troubleshooting as well as improve the security baseline.

To get the most out of visibility, there are a number of principles that must be adhered to in the rest of the environment such as centralised logging and a commitment to truth in reporting.

Everything logs

All systems should produce logs and logs should be used centrally in a system that only categorises the information in the logs at search time. A drawback with the first generation of log management systems was that data was stored in a relational database and that for each device on the network such databases needed a separate table with separate fields. Do not use such a database. Instead, opt for one of the NoSQL options.

Logging is central

All logs should be in a central place, and all devices should have their times synchronized. This is to allow for simultaneous log searches on several devices.

Logging systems do not presume what is in the logs

Ideal logging systems parse the log data at query time and do not rely on pre-sorting and categorization of log fields into predetermined buckets. This allows the security team to investigate at incident time what happened, and does not rely on pre-categorisation of what constitutes a possible event.

All infrastructure and applications have a defined and documented collection approach

The collection strategy specifies what is being logged and why. The main purpose of the collection strategy is to provide some backup in cases of collection *gaps*: systems that should be logging but aren't.

Collection gaps should be filled

Once a collection gap is identified, there is usually no good reason not to fill it. A system that is not logging now, can usually be made to with minimal change.

Operational Security reviews the collection strategy regularly, but not frequently

A collection strategy is a simple strategy that determines which logs are collected, why and how. The collection strategy is driven by knowledge of the effectiveness of certain logs in dealing with particular attacks.

The collection strategy should be visited regularly, but not frequently.

Truth in reporting

Operational security teams can only report truth as they find it. Report data should not be modified to take 'business realities' into account or make uncomfortable truths go away.

The modification of a report is the top of a slippery slope. At the bottom of that slope lies ignorance, the arch enemy of the security team. Do not fall for the temptation.

Insistence should be traceable

Sometimes the security team needs to insist on something getting fixed. It is good to talk about such things, it is better to follow them up in writing. Such insistence should be traceable, either through a trail of written emails or a ticketing system.

Diplomacy is practiced

Diplomacy can be described as the art of getting someone else to do what you need them to do while they think it was their own idea. It is not easy to be a diplomat, and it is not always satisfying.

A risk with a young security capability is that they rush in to look for change by brute force. This rarely works.

Diplomacy practiced by the security team means that an organisation will over time follow the right behaviours without incessant prompting. Instead, the mere fact that problems are visible, as opposed to hidden, will change behaviours.

2

Visibility has its limits

While visibility is a key element of security effectiveness, the visibility that the security team should have in the organisation has its limits. It matters a lot what these limits are and how they are defined. The security team should have enough visibility to do their jobs, but not so much that they become a risk to the organisation. Adherence to the law and policies of the host organisation is also of key importance.

'The law' and policy is a hard limit

The drive to improve visibility in an environment should never be an excuse to break the law or company policy (or both). Things such as privacy and separation of work and personal life do not only exist, they are legal realities and there for a reason.

Enabling invasive monitoring just because it suits the desire of the day is the opposite of good security monitoring. It is creepy, and will destroy trust in the security team in very rapid order. Lost trust of the organisation, lose the security capability itself.

People are a hard limit

Some people cannot, for personal reasons, look at certain things. That is real and valid. Do not ask them to.

'Phishing expeditions' should be discouraged

A security team with good visibility into their environment is sometimes asked to 'go above and beyond' by assisting managers with investigations. If such investigations are sanctioned by HR, meet the relevant laws and are in the best interest of the organisation, proceed and store the relevant paperwork somewhere secure.

If they are not, these things are phishing expeditions which will lose the security team a lot of trust 'on the ground'. Most organisations are rife with gossip, and such events will get out.

The pragmatic solution is to set robust and high bars for such investigations, and not deviate from them.

3

Context: Close the Incident Loop

Incidents are rarely stand-alone. Especially incidents in the Advanced Persistent Threat (APT) category, where the outstanding feature of the attackers is persistence. 'I'll be back' is the catch cry of the APT intruder.

Closing the incident loop means that incidents – especially recurring incidents – are resolved to the point where everything that must be known about an attacker is known.

In intelligence circles, this is called enrichment: combining incident data with other data, or data from previous incidents, to build a more complete picture of the purpose of an attacker.

Understand what success for an attacker looks like

Attackers rarely attack for fun or kicks. In most cases, you are attacked because an attacker wants something. It usually pays to follow the money or data trail, especially for attackers that are seen frequently.

The benefit of understanding an attacker at the 'business' end is significant. It avoids the situation where every incident needs to become an emergency. It allows defenders to distinguish and recognise different attack groups. Identification of 'groups' or actors that are frequently observed on the network, and allows security operations to deal with attacker activities at a coordinated level, especially by breaking the attacker's business model.

Climb the pyramid of pain and block the highest levels

Indicators come in a hierarchy, one that David Bianco has called the pyramid of pain. Blocking attacks higher up the pyramid of pain is better, because the higher you go, the slower an attacker can move. This puts the defender at an advantage.

It is in many cases possible to 'climb the pyramid of pain' and thereby understand the business model of an attacker.

The concept expresses how it is generally difficult, in attack analysis, to move from 'simple indicators' such as file hashes (for weaponised files) to more sophisticated indicators, such as IP addresses and DNS names for Command and Control, to 'Tactics, Techniques and Procedures' (TTPs) – the real business end of a cyber-attack.

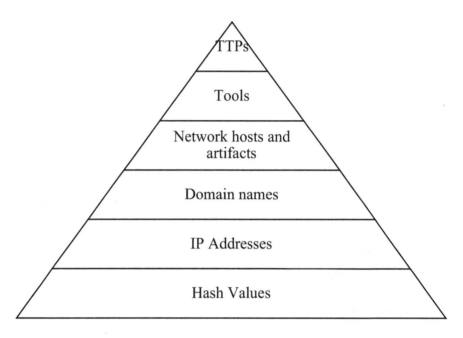

Figure 3.1: The 'pyramid of pain'. At the lower levels, attackers change their appearance rapidly and with little effort. At the higher levels, you enter the 'business model' of the attacker and this is not easily changed. Source: David Bianco: *The Pyramid of Pain*, Blogspot (2013).

Oblique strategies

When the incident response team gets stuck, use oblique strategies to get unstuck. Oblique strategies are cue cards that stimulate tangential thinking in creative processes. There is significant overlap between forming hypotheses about attacker behaviour and creative thinking. The same tools work. Use them.

Break the business model, don't alert on the indicator

Alerting on low level indicators opens an endless 'whack a mole' incident loop, which is ultimately a useless way of dealing with incidents.

Breaking an attack vector on indicators (meaning loading IP addresses into firewalls, or email addresses into email blocks) deals with an incident for only a short time. Good attackers change the lower levels of their attacks like clothes.

The effective way of dealing with a cyberattack is to break the business model of the attacker. Do they sell your information? Ensure your stolen information is worthless by the time it goes up for sale. Does it rely on ransoms being paid? Invest in getting the data back without paying the ransom instead.

Business models are hard to change, and revenue chains are hard to change. This is where attackers are slow moving.

The operative keyword in APT is 'persistent', not 'advanced'

Many people think that the keyword in APT is 'advanced'. It is not. The keyword is 'persistent'. Your APT threats will be seen many times, on a schedule, with an evolving toolset. It pays large dividends to invest in good APT capability for the attackers that are repeatedly after your business and your users.

Another aspect that sets APT attackers apart is long dwell times. APT tooling has a number of characteristics which can be detected by looking consistently and persistently (see principle 1).

Ruthlessly exploit attacker opsec weaknesses

Many attackers are not very good at securing their own operations. This is something that will undoubtedly change in the future, but for now the ease with which many attack operations can be investigated once you know where to look is a large advantage to a defender.

Good defenders know how to exploit the weaknesses in opsec of the attackers to pivot towards other intended victims, infrastructure, and toolsets in use. Toolsets can be investigated further after the attack to determine sophistication and wider relationships in the threat landscape.

Defend your own opsec like a hawk

Weak attacker opsec is no excuse to have weak opsec in the security team. It is sometimes easy to forget that investigating hackers carries some personal risk. Do not expose yourself or your team. Do not use identifiable names.

Investigations use as much as possible the principle of separation and disposable infrastructure. The cloud is ideal for creating and tearing down disposable infrastructure.

Learn how to address uncertainty, urgency, complexity, difficulty and adversity during an incident by building context

Dealing with an incident involves being superior to an attacker on many dimensions. The quickest way to achieve that is by building context around what you see.

Individual alerts triggering on a system of importance create conditions of uncertainty and complexity. Do not overcome this by jumping to conclusions. Stand back and let the facts build the picture. Form hypotheses. Test them.

Attacks are Pareto optimisable

Incidents follow the 80/20 rule. 80% of the incidents on the network are attributable to 20% of the attackers (An expensive way of saying this would be that incidents are Pareto optimisable).

The consequence of this is that the time spent learning how to deal with those 20% of attackers has a large pay-out.

Incidents originating in this group of attackers should be collected in well-documented playbooks and exercised, allowing the lower skilled members of the team to deal with them as part of routine operations, rather than consuming the time and energy of more proficient team members. This allows those team members to focus on the remaining 20% of attacks.

4

Share Aggressively

There is no competitive value in hoarding threat and incident information. Threat information not only can, but should be shared with competitors. Good security teams adhere to standard protocols to facilitate sharing, are part of trust groups to share data, and regularly talk to peers. They put effort into trust groups, and it pays out.

There is no competitive value in attack data

Leaders can be relaxed about sharing most attack data, even down to a deep level, with competitors. There is no competitive value in attack data, except where it may expose details about finances or intellectual property. Most of the time, such information is not important to discuss the details of an attack. You can merely say: the attackers were after intellectual property without disclosing what it is.

Attackers work industry sectors: defenders should too

Attackers tend to work in single industry sectors. This is because many organisations in the same industries use either the same systems, or similar systems. They also use similar processes. Attackers have to spend time building up the picture of their victims, and they can reuse that time and effort by going after many organisations in a single sector of the economy.

The corollary of this is that defenders should also cluster together in industry sectors to better understand attacker patterns and behaviours, and to better understand (probably shared) third party risk.

Attack data combined is more valuable than in isolation

It is only once you start looking beyond individual attacks that attack patterns become obvious. The individual attack will rarely reveal attacker intention, attacker business model or attacker behaviour.

Data gathered from many attacks will display patterns that indicate the behaviour of specific attacker groups.

Take part in the conversation

You only get as much out of the membership of trust groups as you put in. Ever.

5

Do not become a risk yourself

Operational security done well will collect a lot of artefacts that are better not let loose on the network. Have a principle of separation, where such artefacts are kept in a special research network, will enable both safe investigation and avoid the security team becoming a risk to the organisation.

The main purpose of the security operation is to make risks and incidents visible. This should proceed in the following order of preference

1. Logs
2. Read-only system consoles where logs are not available
3. Administrative access where read-only is not available

Separate security operations from the rest

Security operations has a need to delve into things that sometimes better had not touch the business. A separate environment where such investigations can take place is essential for resolving incidents.

Read-only access should be sufficient

For most systems, security only needs to monitor the system but not make actual changes. For most systems, read-only access for the security team should be sufficient. Read-only access also reduces the risks for security operations, because it is not possible to make unauthorised changes to infrastructure and applications.

No admin everywhere

Sometimes security teams believe that they need administrative access to systems in order to monitor them. That is not true. Most systems can be adequately monitored by setting up a robust collection framework and implementing it. That means logging.

For access to consoles, it is possible to set up a 'read only' access in many cases. Only when both are not good enough to monitor an application adequately should administrative access be considered (i.e. not given). This consideration should include an analysis of the benefits of security monitoring versus the costs of the increased attack surface.

Allow admin access only where it makes sense

Some systems need to be administered by security operations, although which systems they are depends on the needs of the organisation.

Then tightly control it

All use of admin accounts should be monitored. Security admin logons from non-security workstations are alerts, not log entries. Admin logons from non-admin workstations are also alerts.

6

Do not start a battle on all fronts

In the initial excitement of gaining visibility into the environment (principle 1) it can be tempting to try and address all problems at once. This is not smart.

Pyrrhic victories are victories without strategic value. Security can end up fighting a lot of battles without strategic value and wear itself out. Having too many battles means the security team is not taken seriously, because no battles ever close.

Choose battles that can be won, and victories worth having. Victories worth having are the ones that have multiple payoffs (better security, stability, less outages, easier to manage), enhance trust between security and the rest of the organisation and form a basis to build on.

Pick the battle as well as the battleground

The strategic questions a security team should be asking before starting to push for security improvements is (i) does having them reduce long-term risk to the business; (ii) does the proposed change have benefits apart from security and (iii) can security be a constructive party in putting the required changes in? Having both (i) and (ii) indicates a problem worth tackling, and having (iii) as well offers a chance to improve the standing of the team.

Having only (i) puts the team at risk of taking the 'department of no' role in the discussion and this has significant reputational cost. This should be considered before taking it on. Having (ii) and (iii) but not (or very little of) (i) is only worth it if there is nothing better to do.

Resource strategic improvements adequately

Improvements that reduce risk, improve aspects other than security and that give the security team a chance to shine are worth resourcing adequately. Do not skimp on the important stuff.

Improve trust in the security team

Security teams that are trusted by their organisations get more done. Trust takes a long time to build and is easily squandered. Making security improvements that reduce risk is good. Making improvements that make everyone's life better is preferable.

Do not win pyrrhic victories

A pyrrhic victory does not reduce long-term risk and has no or few other benefits and is therefore without strategic value. Yet they carry a large cost in terms of security reputation. Pyrrhic victories destroy trust in the security team and have large long-term costs.

7

Security strategy's essence is visibility and context, matched to business value

It is important to have a security strategy. But it is important that strategy stays closely connected to practice. That means strategy must connect means to ends. Strategy that is only strategy mostly does not connect means to ends and is not based on a robust understanding of what an actual attack looks like or does to the business. 'Only strategy' strategy usually substitutes 'best practice' for reality and can be dangerous to adopt.

If there is no information about actual attacks, strategy will most likely be based on perceptions and politics and will achieve the status of fairy tales at best. This is not a good basis to run security operations from.

When considering strategy, there is 'grand strategy' and 'operational strategy'. Grand strategy is compelling, connects means to ends, and considers the possible, but in terms meaningful to the business. Operational strategy considers what you would do in a given (possibly imagined) situation and is actionable.

Do not conflate the two.

Both are equally important. Grand strategy imaginings without operational strategic counterparts are useless.

Grand security strategy is measurable

Real strategy is based on understanding, context and quantification of business risks into a security context, and always matches means to ends. Better strategy also has narrative and is compelling. Superior strategy has all these properties and is moreover continuously visible and measurable.

Grand security strategy connects to the business

Grand security strategy talks about possible impacts of cyber security events to real business events. It is not system based.

'Possible' scenarios are good. Actual scenarios are better. Actual (but limited in scope) scenarios can be extended to possible, larger scope scenarios by running through the chain of events and imagining one or more security controls failed. While that did not happen last time, it can do so in the future.

Sound operational strategy is actionable

From the viewpoint of security operations, strategy initiatives should ensure visibility into the environment with a fighting chance to build context.

Attack data, as far as available, plays a key role in this. Once an organisation has successfully dealt with several attacks, the next target of strategy is to make it 'bottom up' – based on actual attack data. 'Visibility everywhere (principle 1), 'context' (principle 3) and the scope of action (principles 5 and 6) should always be the main drivers of operational strategy.

Robust operational strategy begins with pushing for better visibility and resources to establish context, and then turns that insight into action.

This is what closing the incident loop all is about: learning from incidents to a level where it becomes possible to permanently immunise the organisation against attacks of a certain kind. Strategy then moves the organisation on to the next kind.

'Risk' is risk to business processes and revenue, not systems

In the context of a running business, systems mean little, whereas processes and revenue are meaningful quantities. If you can only link risks to systems, ask more questions of the business to understand where and how these systems are important to the whole.

'Risk' is only a substitute

An organisation that has no actual attack data and no means to get it should use a risk calculation to build a case for visibility tooling and resourcing to get context. Very little else matters.

It can be tempting to do 'strategy' based on best practice and generic boilerplate gratuitously delivered by consultants or downloaded from the internet. Do this if you must, but realise that 'best practice' is seldom strategic, and boilerplate rarely actionable.

Strategy tells a story

Both also miss one other crucial component of strategy. Good strategy must be compelling. 'Best practice' and boilerplate are not inspiring goals to strive for.

Good strategy is not only compelling in its ends, but matches means to ends. Gaining better visibility into the environment is compelling not only from the viewpoint of improved security, but also from the viewpoint of system reliability and predictability.

It is also doable: most modern systems have robust logging capabilities and when all else fails, logs are a good point to start from. Most organisations already run antivirus. When was the last time someone looked at its dashboards?

Strategy based on 'risk' is OK, strategy based on actual facts is much better

'Risk' is often perceived and rarely measured. Strategy based on perceived risk will not achieve much. Strategy based on risk that's measured and understood is priceless.

Improvements in the visibility and context will allow an organisation to quantify and contextualise risk. As a result, conversations about cyber strategy at board level will be meaningful.

Define scope, time and space

Key operational strategic concerns are scope, time and space. Scope is the range of allowable actions.

A security strategy should be, and can be, precisely scoped. This is important for the aspects of sharing (principle 4), as well as setting out the rights and obligations of security operations to the range of business processes and suppliers.

Time defines incident response as a service. While it is not possible to set SLAs on forensics, it is possible to set SLAs to some degree on incident containment, provided the team dealing with the incident has a defined scope of action. This is because actions can be time-boxed. E.g. can they turn that web server off?

Space defines the constituency of the security team. Who are they acting for?

Part III

Summary

In highly unpredictable situations like cyber incidents, responders face a dangerous cocktail of uncertainty, urgency, adversarial behaviour, complexity and volatility. In such situations, I believe it is better to be grounded in a robust set of principles than to make it up as you go. This small book has outlined the principles that have worked for me and my teams in the past.

'Making it up' may be acceptable in the normal course of events. But things radically change when organisations are under attack or dealing with fallout of a serious incident.

During incident time, 'making it up' is a risky strategy that, when confronted with the realities of a cyber-incident, exposes teams to undue political pressure, and downright organisational incompetence. This leads to inconsistent approaches to incidents and attackers, all of which lead to an undesirable increase in uncertainty, pressure and burnout.

Consistent approaches are based on services. For a team with principles, incident response is a service, and should be, as much as possible, repeatable, with defined targets for containment of the incident. When an incident response plan exists, containment consists of discrete actions that can be time-boxed. Beyond containment, SLAs cannot be defined.

To promote use, I have tried to make my statement of principles brief and concise. They should be usable and referenceable under pressure. It should be possible, in the heat of the moment, to take a step back and confirm a principle before an action is taken.

With that, this statement of principles is somewhat personal. They are the principles that have worked for me in the past. I may have missed some. At that point, create your own. This book is a work in progress above all else.

List of principles

Visibility: Go by what there is, not by what there should be

Everything is visible and measurable

All infrastructure and applications have a defined and documented collection approach

Truth in reporting

Insistence should be traceable

Diplomacy is practiced

Visibility has its limits

'The law' and policy is a hard limit

People are a hard limit

'Phishing expeditions' should be discouraged

Context: Close the Incident Loop

Understand what success for an attacker looks like

Climb the pyramid of pain and block the highest levels

Oblique strategies

Break the business model, don't alert on the indicator

The operative keyword in APT is 'persistent', not 'advanced'

Ruthlessly exploit attacker opsec weaknesses

Defend your own opsec like a hawk

Learn how to address uncertainty, urgency, complexity, difficulty and adversity during an incident by building context

Attacks are Pareto optimisable

Share Aggressively

There is no competitive value in attack data

Attackers work industry sectors: defenders should too

Attack data combined is more valuable than in isolation

Take part in the conversation

Do not become a risk yourself

Separate security operations from the rest

Read-only access should be sufficient

No admin everywhere

Allow admin access only where it makes sense

Then tightly control it

Do not start a battle on all fronts

Pick the battle as well as the battleground

Resource strategic improvements adequately

Improve trust in the security team

Do not win pyrrhic victories

Security strategy's essence is visibility and context, matched to business value

Grand security strategy is measurable

Grand security strategy connects to the business

Sound operational strategy is actionable

'Risk' is risk to business processes and revenue, not systems

'Risk' is only a substitute

Strategy tells a story

Strategy based on 'risk' is OK, strategy based on actual facts is much better

Define scope, time and space

Notes and References

Why principles?

Reading Ray Dalio's book *'Principles'* (Simon & Schuster, 2017), it struck me that security operations follows a set of principles of its own. This book is merely my attempt to write them down.

Dalio outlines a lot of the reasoning why principles are important in general and why and how they matter, and inspired me to start documenting the ones that I believe are important for security operations.

Dalio's first principle: 'think for yourself to decide what you want, what is true, and what you should do to achieve what you want in the light of what is true' is also very much in operation in this book.

General background to security operations

This book talks about principles and stays away from specific practices and tools, let alone product and vendors.

A lot has already been written about security operations, and more is discovered daily. Personally, I find Carson Zimmerman's (free) book *'10 strategies for a world class cybersecurity operations center'* (MITRE, 2014) one of the best.

A copy is available here:

https://www.mitre.org/publications/all/ten-strategies-of-a-world-class-cybersecurity-operations-center

The pyramid of pain is now a quite well-known concept. It was, to my knowledge, first introduced in a blog post by David Bianco in 2013:

http://detect-respond.blogspot.com/2013/03/the-pyramid-of-pain.html

Oblique Strategies

Oblique strategies is a collection of cards that are designed to promote tangential thinking. When stuck, draw a card. A deck is available for purchase on https://www.enoshop.co.uk/product/oblique-strategies.html

There are also online or printable versions. When stuck, draw a card.

Ethics and behaviours

This book outlines operational principles and does not really talk about ethics and what is right and wrong in incident response. A working group of first.org has recently done some work on that topic:

https://www.first.org/global/sigs/ethics/ethics-first

www.ingramcontent.com/pod-product-compliance
Lightning Source LLC
Chambersburg PA
CBHW031232050326
40689CB00009B/1568